Original title:

Gnarled Crowns Among the Wizard Fence

Copyright © 2025 Swan Charm

Author: Kene Elistrand

ISBN HARDBACK: 978-1-80559-497-0

ISBN PAPERBACK: 978-1-80559-996-8

An Odyssey Beneath the Overgrown Canopy

In shadows deep, where secrets creep,
Dappled light through leaves does seep.
Ancient roots that twist and wind,
Whispers of the past unwind.

Mossy stones and fragrant air,
Every step, a tale laid bare.
Ferns unfurl in emerald grace,
Time has paused in this sacred space.

Amongst the branches, creatures dwell,
Their stories shared, a silent spell.
Echoes of the wild unfold,
Nature's wonder, fierce and bold.

With every breath, the forest sighs,
Beneath the vast and watchful skies.
A winding path, a journey vast,
In the embrace of trees steadfast.

Through tangled vines and misty dreams,
Life flows softly, like gentle streams.
In the realm where shadows roam,
The earth reveals its timeless home.

The Arboreal Scribes' Legacy

In the heart of the grove, secrets dwell,
Whispers of ancient trees weave a spell.
Leaves turn pages in the bright sunlight,
Stories of old, they dance in flight.

Roots dig deep in the sacred ground,
Silent watchers, they hear no sound.
Branches stretch wide with a knowing grace,
Guardians of wisdom, they find their place.

Season by season, they tell their lore,
Carved in the bark, forevermore.
A tapestry woven with time and care,
Nature's own scribes in the cool, fresh air.

From acorn to oak, they rise and grow,
Echoes of legends in every blow.
The sun sets low, the shadows blend,
The legacy lives on, it will not end.

Beneath the stars, their stories gleam,
In the whispering winds, we hear them dream.
The arboreal scribes with silent sighs,
Link past and present under vast skies.

Vines of the Forgotten

In a forgotten garden, vines entwine,
Whispers of secrets in each design.
Shadows creep softly as dusk descends,
Silent embrace where the old path bends.

Colors of dusk as the daylight fades,
In shadows and light, an ancient cascade.
Curled around pillars of stone and dust,
Nature's embrace, in her we trust.

Leaves once lush, now a muted hue,
Stories hidden in the morning dew.
Each tendril's journey, a tale untold,
In nature's arms, the mysteries unfold.

Wandering spirits in twilight's glow,
Vines reach out where the memories flow.
A touch of the past in every embrace,
The garden whispers of time's gentle grace.

In twilight's dance, they sway and weave,
For those who linger, and dare believe.
Vines of the forgotten, with magic in hand,
Carry the tales of this timeless land.

Enchanted Shadows Embrace

Beneath the eaves where the twilight spills,
Shadows embrace with a touch of thrills.
In the glens where moonlight bends,
Magic awakens and softly transcends.

Whispers float on the cool night air,
Dreams take flight in a world so rare.
Leaves tremble lightly, a melodic sigh,
As the stars wink down from the velvet sky.

Allies of darkness in soft, gentle hues,
The forest gleams with the night's subtle clues.
Footsteps echo on the worn, soft trail,
Stories of wonder in every pale veil.

With every rustle, the night unfolds,
Dancing in shadows, the secret holds.
Creatures emerge from their hidden nooks,
Each one diving into enchanted books.

In the heart of the night where magic weaves,
A sanctuary born from the dreams it retrieves.
Enchanted shadows, forever embraced,
In the depths of the woods, we find our place.

The King's Folly in the Woods

In the shadows deep, the king lost his way,
Through tangled paths where the wild things play.
His crown, once bright, now heavy with threat,
Regrets linger on, like the sun's last set.

Riches he sought in the emerald mire,
With each step forward, his heart lost fire.
In the heart of the woods, illusions deceive,
A throne veiled by shadows, where wise men grieve.

The laughter of sprites, the murmur of trees,
Echoed like memories carried by breeze.
A folly of power, so brief and so grand,
Now buried in silence, the king's own hand.

From gilded halls to the world of the meek,
He sought fleeting glory but found only bleak.
In the deep of the forest, where secrets conspire,
He learned of true worth, not gold or desire.

As dawn breaks anew, he steps forth as one,
A humbled ruler, his old battles won.
The woods have their wisdom, ancient and bold,
The king's folly taught him what dreams uphold.

Twisted Regality of the Ancients

In the halls where echoes throng,
Ghostly whispers weave their song.
Crowned in thorns, they reign sublime,
Beneath the weight of ancient time.

Faded banners, torn and frayed,
Tales of glory, long betrayed.
Chiseled faces, wrought of stone,
Guard the secrets of the throne.

Flickering candles, shadows dance,
Lost in whispers of romance.
Chambered hearts hold tales untold,
As the twilight turns to gold.

Riddles carved in marble pride,
Speak of glory and the tide.
Regal dreams entwined with fate,
Pillars crumbling, enhance the weight.

Time's cruel hand, it bends the crown,
Turning majesty to frown.
In the ruins, a silent plea,
Echoes of what used to be.

Shadows of the Forbidden Thicket

In the thicket, shadows creep,
Secrets buried, lost in sleep.
Leaves that whisper, tales of yore,
Of forgotten myths and lore.

Branches twist in solemn dance,
Inviting thoughts of lost romance.
Dappled light, in fleeting beams,
Glimmers softly on the dreams.

Footfalls echo, lightly tread,
In the path where few have fled.
Curious eyes, the woods entice,
Revealing truths, but at a price.

Moonlit glades, where spirits roam,
Cradle hearts, that seek a home.
Veils of mist, and shadows blend,
In the darkness, truths extend.

Caught in webs of twilight's grace,
Nature's heart, a vivid place.
In the silence, whispers say,
Find the light within the gray.

Mysterious Roots Beneath the Spellbound Boughs

Beneath the boughs where magic sighs,
Roots entangle, truth belies.
Woven tales in twisted form,
Nurtured in the quiet storm.

Gnarled fingers, touch the earth,
Cradling whispers of rebirth.
Deep below, the secrets dwell,
Silent stories, cast a spell.

In the glen, where shadows loom,
Fleeting glimpses of the gloom.
Nature's heart beats slow and deep,
Guarding dreams that dare to leap.

Vines that hold the skies so tight,
Caught in dance of day and night.
Each breath taken, souls entwined,
In the roots, true love confined.

Will you wander through the mist?
Past the trees, do not resist.
For beneath the sacred ground,
Hidden truths shall be found.

Thorns Fashioned by Time's Hand

In the garden where thorns do grow,
Time has shaped each silent foe.
Petals fade, their hues decay,
Echoing the price we pay.

Barbed memories wound the heart,
Crafted by each tear that starts.
Yet in pain, there blooms a rose,
Beauty thrives where sorrow sows.

Twisting paths of dark and light,
Guide the way through endless night.
Each thorn a badge, each scar a tale,
Whispers linger, soft and frail.

Seasons change, the cycle spins,
New growth rises from what's been.
In the garden, life expands,
Fashioned by time's gentle hands.

Hold fast to all the beauty found,
In the thorns that intertwine the ground.
For in the struggle, strength we gain,
From love's embrace, we bear the strain.

The Secret Feasts of Midnight Crows

Beneath the stars, their banquet glows,
Amidst the shadows, the darkness flows.
A feast of whispers, secrets shared,
The crows await, the night prepared.

With glistening eyes, they gather near,
A chorus of caws, the sound we fear.
They dance on winds, their wings aflame,
In twilight's hush, they chant their name.

Old tales of magic, lost in time,
Each morsel savored, a silent rhyme.
Their midnight feasts, a sight bestowed,
The secrets spun, tales long ago.

And as the moon begins to wane,
The crows depart, but not in vain.
For every night, they will return,
With stories learned and lessons earned.

So heed the calls, when darkness sighs,
For in their flight, the truth implies.
The night is rich, with voices low,
In whispered tones, the crows bestow.

Whispers from the Eldritch Garden

In shadows deep, the blooms arise,
With colors bright, beneath dark skies.
The garden breathes, a mystic air,
Where whispers weave, and secrets dare.

The vines entwine, in eerie grace,
Each petal holds a timeless trace.
An ancient song, so softly sung,
In every leaf, old tales are hung.

The moonlight kisses, the blooms unfold,
Revealing mysteries, dark and bold.
With every gust, the spirits hum,
In this strange place, the night feels numb.

Beware the path where shadows loom,
For lost are those who dare to roam.
Yet still they come, those brave of heart,
To kiss the night and play their part.

So linger close to nature's spell,
In whispers soft, the stories dwell.
For in this garden, dark and vast,
The present meets the ancient past.

Enigma of the Wreathed Branches

Beneath the trees where shadows creep,
An enigma hides, in silence deep.
Wreathed branches twist, with secrets bound,
In fractured light, the answers found.

A tapestry of leaves unfurled,
Whispers of magic from another world.
The winds conspire, and time stands still,
In this bizarre realm, we meet the will.

With every rustle, a story brews,
Of olden times, forgotten clues.
The heart of nature beats anew,
As branches bend, and spirits view.

So journey close, to where they reign,
In cryptic shadows, both wild and sane.
The enigma waits for those who seek,
For in their arms, the truths do speak.

And when you gaze on branches wreathed,\nKnow there's
a world that's not unscathed.
For in the dark, the light shall weave,
A tale of all who dare believe.

Nightfall's Crowning Enchantment

As day concedes to night's embrace,
An enchantment stirs, adorned in grace.
The twilight paints the sky anew,
In shades of indigo, deep and true.

Stars awaken, a flicker bright,
Each one a beacon, in the night.
A crown of jewels on velvet skies,
Whispers of dreams, in lullabies.

The moon ascends, a silver queen,
Cloaked in mystery, softly seen.
She bears the tales of love and woe,
In gentle beams, her secrets glow.

With every breeze, the night reveals,
The magic spun that time conceals.
A dance of shadows, soft and sweet,
In night's embrace, our hearts repeat.

And as we breathe this wondrous air,
In moments rare, we shed our care.
For nightfall grants us soft ascent,
To realms where dreams and wonders blend.

Whispers of Twisted Majesty

In twilight's glow, the shadows sway,
A crown of thorns marks the passing day.
Beneath the sky, the whispers rise,
With secrets held in twilight's sighs.

The gnarled branches weave their tale,
A dance of leaves where echoes sail.
The twilight mist wraps round so tight,
As stars appear to pierce the night.

A regal moon crowns the darkened wood,
Where ancient spirits have always stood.
They speak of dreams long lost, yet true,
In mysteries spun from twilight's hue.

Through twisted paths, the echoes call,
In whispered tones that rise and fall.
Majesty lurks in every bend,
A truth revealed, as shadows blend.

As darkness folds, the night takes flight,
With tales of love and ancient might.
The heart of the forest beats so strong,
In twisted majesty, we belong.

Enchanted Thorns and Shadowed Realms

Through thickets deep, the thorns embrace,
An enchanted tale in a hidden space.
Beneath the arch of yearning trees,
The shadows dance with whispered pleas.

In realms where sunlight seldom breaks,
Silent magic stirs and wakes.
With every step, a story sown,
In tangled roots, our fright is grown.

The thorns entwine like fate's cruel touch,
Yet in the binds, we feel so much.
A love forbidden, fierce, and true,
In shadowed realms, we find our hue.

Echoes linger, stories paved,
In thorns of night, the hearts are saved.
Together woven, in shadows' ranks,
We find our strength amid the pranks.

With every turn, the night unveils,
The passion masked beneath the trails.
In enchanted thorns, our hearts entwine,
In shadowed realms, the world resigns.

The Crow's Conspiracy at Dusk

Beneath the trees where shadows fall,
Crows gather round, a secret call.
With coal-black wings against the sky,
They scheme and plot as dusk draws nigh.

In whispered tones, they share their tales,
Of ancient paths and midnight trails.
The wisdom of the lost and found,
In every crow's haunting sound.

With watchful eyes, they know the game,
In shadows cloaked, they stake their claim.
A silent pact, a flight of fate,
In conspiracies that never wait.

At dusk's embrace, the darkness swells,
With secrets shared and whispered spells.
The world below fades from view,
As crows unite in shades of blue.

Through brooding skies, their voices blend,
In cawing tones, our fears suspend.
The crow's conspiracy unfolds with grace,
In dusk's embrace, we find our place.

Hallowed Vines in the Enchanted Glade

In hallowed vines, the secrets twine,
Within the glade, where whispers shine.
A realm of dreams, both bright and dim,
Where nature sings a timeless hymn.

The footfalls soft on carpeted earth,
Breathe in the air, feel the rebirth.
With every glance, the heart ignites,
In sacred spaces, magic ignites.

Beneath the boughs, the shadows play,
In laughter's song, we drift away.
The vines entwined in tender grip,
Guide us along this wondrous trip.

As twilight falls, the fireflies gleam,
Painting the night with a glowing dream.
A sacred weave of light and shade,
In hallowed vines, our hearts cascaded.

Through the glade, a promise flows,
Of memories sweet as the evening glows.
In laughter shared, in whispers made,
We'll find our truth in the enchanted glade.

Veils of Fog and Forgotten Lore

In the early dawn, whispers glide,
Veils of fog cloak the silent tide.
Winds of secrets weave through trees,
Cradling tales on autumn's breeze.

Mossy stones and shadowed paths,
Carry echoes of ancient laughs.
Where time's river softly flows,
In haze the history quietly grows.

Chasing memories on wings of night,
Dim lanterns flicker in fading light.
A compass lost, yet hearts take flight,
To seek the past, to find what's right.

Here the fabric of dreams entwine,
With threads of fate and aged pine.
In every layer of mist's embrace,
Lies forgotten lore, a sacred space.

So linger here where shadows play,
Unravel treasures before they sway.
For in the fog, the stories lie,
And those who seek shall hear the sigh.

The Whispering Thicket's Lament

In thickets deep, where dreams reside,
The whispers dance, the shadows hide.
Each rustling leaf, a tale untold,
Of hearts once brave, now faint and cold.

Moonlight bathes the forest's floor,
Echoing soft, the thicket's lore.
A lament low, a haunting tune,
Played by the night, beneath the moon.

Tangled branches reach for stars,
Each scarred bough hides silent scars.
In the quiet, the thicket weeps,
For memories lost, for promises it keeps.

With every sigh, the shadows creep,
Stirring soul's depths from peaceful sleep.
Here longing lingers, shadows entwine,
A symphony forged in nature's design.

So wander slow, let silence guide,
In the whispering thicket, secrets bide.
What nature shares is often rare,
The lament whispers, if you're aware.

Elegy for the Crowned Creatures

In twilight's glow, they roam the glades,
Crowned in dreams where twilight fades.
Whispers of glory, shadows of grace,
Elegies linger in their space.

Among the wild, the regal stride,
Yet time encroaches, with steady tide.
Once vibrant hearts and spirits bold,
Now echoes of stories, softly told.

With antlers high, they tread the dawn,
On paths once bright, now nearly gone.
Each thrum of life, a bittersweet song,
In nature's court, they still belong.

Moonlit nights beckon their song,
Yet omens whisper, something's wrong.
Each call of night, a mournful sound,
For crowned creatures, forever bound.

In sylvan halls, their echoes dwell,
A solemn tale, a silent bell.
For as they fade into the dark,
The woods remember, each sacred spark.

Through the Eyes of the Bewitched Foliage

Through emerald leaves, the stories weave,
In shadows thick where spirits cleave.
Glimmers of magic, wild and free,
The foliage whispers, come and see.

Gnarled branches twist in graceful dance,
As fairies play in their sweet romance.
Every rustle, a spell that's cast,
Binding the future to the past.

In the dappled light of a sunbeam's gaze,
The heart of the forest begins to blaze.
With colors bright, enchantments bloom,
Through bewitched foliage, escape the gloom.

Ancient roots hold deep the lore,
Of timeless wonders forevermore.
A gaze through leaves, brings visions true,
Of realms where dreams and hopes renew.

So linger softly, listen near,
Through every shiver, every cheer.
For in their eyes, magic resides,
Through the foliage, the heart confides.

Crowned Nightmares of Forgotten Kings

Beneath the stars, shadows creep,
Silent whispers, secrets deep.
A throne of ash, a faded dream,
In twilight's grasp, lost kings scream.

Their crowns now rust, memories choke,
In shattered halls, an ancient cloak.
Echoes howl through the barren night,
A haunting dance, devoid of light.

They held the power, they held the might,
Yet trust betrayed, turned dark the light.
Faded portraits, staring still,
Mark the echoes of broken will.

Crowned in fate, yet lost to time,
Their stories dimmed, a mournful rhyme.
In tales unwoven, shadows dwell,
Forgotten kings in a dying hell.

The Fabled Path of Elderlore

Twisted roots and ancient stones,
A pathway whispers of long-lost thrones.
Beneath the boughs, the stories hide,
Their tales of magic, a river wide.

Through time-worn trails and misty dreams,
The fabled path sews silver seams.
In shadows thick, the spirits weave,
A tapestry for those who believe.

With every step, the echoes call,
A siren's song to one and all.
By lantern's glow, the wisdom flows,
In Elderlore, the heart still knows.

The journey bends, the night grows old,
In whispered lore, the truth is told.
Find magic here, where stories blend,
On the fabled path, where wisdom transcends.

Enchantment in Every Crinkle

A paper map with edges worn,
Holds tales of magic, old and torn.
In crinkles deep, enchantments dwell,
Secrets whispered, words to spell.

With every fold, a journey starts,
Adventures spun from aching hearts.
Through valleys lush and mountains high,
In every crease, a chance to fly.

The parchment's touch, a timeless thread,
Leads wanderers where dreams have led.
From inked lines, the visions spring,
Awakening the hope they bring.

In every crinkle, stories hide,
Ancient journeys, paths that bide.
Unfold the magic, let it soar,
In every crack, there's something more.

Lore about Roots and Realms

In gardens lush, the roots entwine,
Connecting worlds, a hidden sign.
From earth's embrace, old stories rise,
In tales unspoken, truth belies.

Realms above and realms below,
Interwoven, seeds we sow.
With roots that dig and branches soar,
We find the tales that we adore.

Each leaf a whisper, each stem a thread,
Connecting realms where angels tread.
In every bloom, a secret's cast,
The lore of life, both vast and fast.

Echoing through the whispered glades,
In shadows deep, the magic wades.
Roots that hold, and realms that meet,
Where legends live, and time's heartbeat.

Bound by Nature's Will

In the forest deep and wide,
Whispers of the trees abide.
Roots entwined in ancient lore,
Nature's rhythms we explore.

Rivers flow with endless grace,
Carving paths, they find their place.
Mountains tall in silence stand,
Guardians of this sacred land.

Underneath the twilight sky,
Stars awaken, dreams will fly.
Beasts and blooms in concert sing,
Harmony that earth will bring.

Seasons dance in vibrant hues,
Painting tales in shades and views.
Bound by nature's gentle thread,
Life unfolds where dreams are fed.

In this realm, we find our way,
Every breath a soft ballet.
Bound by nature's timeless will,
In her arms, our hearts are still.

The Warden's Wildwood

Through the thickets, shadows creep,
Warden guards the woods so deep.
Ancient oak and silver birch,
Whisper secrets as they lurch.

In the glen where wildflowers bloom,
Life awakens, dispelling gloom.
Creatures scurry, branches sway,
Living tales of night and day.

Moonlight bathes the forest floor,
Echoes linger, spirits soar.
Each step echoes in the night,
Warden watches, hidden from sight.

In the heart of wildwood's might,
Nature's magic, pure delight.
Bound to time, yet always new,
Warden's oath, forever true.

Through the dark, the dawn will break,
Awakening the dreams we make.
In this sanctuary's embrace,
Warden's wildwood, sacred space.

Fences of Time and Enchantment

In the meadow where time stands still,
Fences guard the magic's thrill.
Moments weave like silken thread,
Stories linger, never fled.

Whispers float on autumn's breeze,
Memories dance among the trees.
Each sunset paints a tale untold,
In twilight's grasp, the world is gold.

Fences crafted with love and care,
Hold enchantments hidden there.
Glimmers of a past embraced,
Every heartbeat truly traced.

Time meanders, swift yet slow,
In its grasp, the wonders grow.
Life's sweet moments, cherished tight,
Enchantment's glow in soft moonlight.

So let us wander, hand in hand,
Through this realm, we'll make our stand.
Fences of time and dreams will bind,
A world of magic, intertwined.

Veins of Verdant Magic

In the heart of emerald glades,
Veins of magic softly cascade.
Leaves like whispers, tales unfold,
Secrets hidden, stories told.

Beneath the boughs of ancient trees,
Nature breathes in gentle ease.
Streams like ribbons, clear and bright,
Flowing softly in the night.

Petals drift on summer's air,
Breezes carry scents so rare.
Life ignites in colors bold,
Veins of magic, vibrant gold.

Every creature finds its place,
In this realm of wild embrace.
In the thicket, dreams take flight,
Veins of magic, pure delight.

So let us wander, hearts set free,
In this tapestry, you and me.
Nature's pulse, forever near,
Veins of verdant magic here.

Thickets of Sorcery and Secrets

In shadows deep the whispers weave,
Ancient spells the night does cleave.
Thickets thick with secrets' breath,
In every rustle lies a death.

Moonlit paths where fairies dance,
Mystic runes enhance their chance.
Glimmers fade in evening's glow,
Magic stirs in thickets low.

The wind carries a daydream's sigh,
Voices linger, soft and spry.
Each step taken echoes fate,
In these woods, too soon, too late.

Vines entwined with fate's own thread,
Stories linger where they tread.
In tangled roots and branches wide,
The heart of magic must abide.

Mysteries whispered, hearts ablaze,
Caught within enchantment's haze.
Thickets guard the truth so dear,
Secrets wait when night draws near.

Eclipsed by Arcane Overgrowth

Beneath the canopy so thick,
Magic pulses, shadows flick.
Evergreen with secrets deep,
In silence, ancient spirits creep.

The moon's glow filters, soft and pale,
Each sound carries a hidden tale.
Eclipsed by foliage, time stands still,
In every rustle lies a thrill.

Gnarled roots that twist and turn,
In their embrace, new dreams will burn.
Whispers flow like streams of light,
Guiding lost souls through the night.

Flickering shadows sway and spin,
Calling forth the magic within.
The forest breathes a breath of fate,
Every pulse, every gate.

A tapestry of bark and vine,
Secrets stitch a grand design.
Arcane echoes, timeless, true,
In the overgrowth, we renew.

The Chronicles of the Enchanted Grove

Hidden paths where fables grow,
Chronicles in the twilight glow.
Every leaf tells tales of yore,
Of love and loss, of myths and lore.

In the grove, enchantments play,
Where shadows fade but never stray.
The heart of magic beats so clear,
In every branch, in every tear.

Glistening streams through woodland roam,
Whispered secrets find their home.
Time entwined in nature's weave,
In the grove, we dare believe.

Winds sing soft, a lullaby,
Underneath the starry sky.
Chronicles alive with song,
Where the lost and found belong.

An invitation to the brave,
In the grove, life's moments save.
Here, where wonder knows no end,
Every heart finds a friend.

Unseen Monarchs of the Twilight Wood

In twilight's hush, the unseen reign,
Monarchs dance without a chain.
Majestic spirits, veiled in mist,
In every sigh, the night is kissed.

Branches bow to ancient might,
Filling the air with pure delight.
In shadows deep, their secrets swirl,
Magic thrives in every whirl.

Through tangled paths, the echoes flow,
Guided by the moon's warm glow.
A kingdom hidden, vast and grand,
Where unseen monarchs make their stand.

Stars above like chandeliers bright,
Illuminating hidden flight.
The wood alive with softest sound,
In their presence, magic's found.

Veils of twilight, whispers sweet,
Unseen monarchs, in retreat.
Guardians of this sacred place,
In every breath, they leave their trace.

Enchanted Briars and Starlit Halls

In shadows deep, where whispers play,
The briars dance in moonlit sway,
A soft lament, a tender call,
In starlit dreams within these halls.

Crimson blooms beneath the night,
Fairy lights in gentle flight,
They weave a tale that pulls you near,
As magic brews and hearts draw clear.

With every step, a secret found,
Where time and space twist all around,
The echoes sing of ancient lore,
Inviting you to seek and explore.

Here love and fate entwined shall roam,
In briars' grasp, we find our home,
Amidst the stars that fell like rain,
In starlit halls, our dreams remain.

Dreams Entangled in a Forest of Whimsy

In the forest where dreams collide,
Whimsy laughs and shadows bide,
With every leaf that twirls and spins,
A tapestry of where love begins.

Colorful sprites in playful flight,
Chasing whispers, veiling light,
Each corner holds a brand new tale,
In this sanctuary, none can fail.

Mossy beds and crystal streams,
We wander through our woven dreams,
Each gaze a spark, each touch a flame,
In such a place, we play the game.

Time drifts softly, like the breeze,
Among the branches, between the trees,
With open hearts, we dare to pause,
Embracing all that wonder draws.

So dance with me on twilight's edge,
Through whimsy's path, we make our pledge,
To chase the stories through the night,
In dreams entangled, pure delight.

Eldritch Groves and Hidden Realms

In eldritch groves where shadows loom,
Ancient whispers birth their bloom,
Hidden realms of twilight's grace,
A secret world, a sacred space.

Eerie lights in forests dense,
A mystic call, a deep suspense,
With every step, the magic seeps,
Into the heart, where silence keeps.

Veils of mist in soft embrace,
Entwined in dreams, we seek a trace,
Of visions bold, of wonders rare,
In hidden realms, beyond compare.

Gnarled branches twist and sigh,
As shadows dance beneath the sky,
With echoes drawn from ancient lore,
We find our path, we seek for more.

In eldritch groves, where stories start,
We forge the magic in our heart,
For every step in realms unknown,
Brings forth the seeds of dreams we've sown.

Echoes of the Enchanted Arbour

In the arbour where echoes dwell,
A whispered tale, a woven spell,
With branches twined and flowers bright,
We listen close to nature's light.

Each breeze that stirs the silent leaves,
Carries with it the dreams that weave,
Around our hearts, they gently twine,
In enchanted moments, so divine.

As twilight brings a soft embrace,
We watch the stars begin to trace,
A path of hope across the skies,
In the arbour, where magic lies.

With every heartbeat, time stands still,
In the embrace of nature's will,
The echoes hum a sweet refrain,
Reminding us where love remains.

In the enchanted arbour's glow,
We plant the seeds of dreams to grow,
With echoes rich, we weave our song,
In harmony where we belong.

The Crown's Quiet Conspiracy

A throne sits still in shadowed halls,
Where silence drapes like velvet falls.
Whispers crawl through gilded doors,
Secrets held in silence, scores.

Beneath the weight of silent crowns,
The dreams of kings slip slowly down.
In chambers where the echoes sigh,
Ambitions rise, and loyalties die.

Veiled plots weave through the night,
In candle's glow, a ghostly light.
Trust dances on a fragile thread,
In every glance, the silence spreads.

Each secret passed like poisoned wine,
Hides the truth, a dangerous line.
Old bonds break in the darkened scheme,
While fate weaves softly, a clever dream.

In twilight's grasp, conspirators play,
The crown's quiet game leads hearts astray.
Yet amidst the shadows, truth may bloom,
For even whispers can shatter gloom.

Secrets Held within the Bark

In ages past, the trees did sigh,
Holding whispers from on high.
Deep within their ancient rings,
Secrets dance on gentle wings.

Each knot and twist a tale concealed,\nIn wood's embrace,
truths revealed.
The sap flows thick with stories old,
In every grain, a truth untold.

Leaves rustle soft, an echoed laugh,
Nature's pen writes history's path.
Roots intertwine with love and fear,
In every shadow, a dream draws near.

The canopy blocks the sunlit gleam,
Yet through the bark, life's secrets stream.
A silent witness to the years,
With every sigh, it holds our tears.

As seasons turn and time unspools,
The forest breathes, keeping its rules.
In every whisper of the breeze,
Lies the knowledge of ancient trees.

The Glade of Bewitched Echoes

In twilight's grip, the glade appears,
Where laughter mingles with uncried tears.
Echoes swell like shadows cast,
In the heart of woods, time holds fast.

A haunting breeze through boughs will weave,
Waking dreams that we believe.
Soft murmurs dance like fireflies,
And secrets twinkle in the skies.

Among the ferns, enchantments creep,
Awakening the night from sleep.
In the stillness, magic thrives,
A symphony of whispered lives.

Each footstep stirs the silken air,
Flashing glimpses of wonders rare.
In this glade where echoes play,
The past and present swirl away.

When night falls deep, the stars align,
In their glow, the world divine.
In this haven, hope's embrace,
The glade spins tales, a sacred space.

Tales Whispered on the Wind's Breath

The wind carries stories far and wide,
With every gust, dreams coincide.
In the rustling leaves, tales unfold,
Of love, loss, and legends bold.

From mountain peaks to ocean's edge,
Each whisper treads a sacred pledge.
The breath of nature sings its song,
In every note, where souls belong.

Skies reveal what hearts conceal,
With every sigh, the truth will feel.
Time bends softly round each plea,
As the wind embraces you and me.

Across the fields, the echoes glide,
Through valleys wide, they dance and bide.
In every turn, the stories blend,
Curving paths that never end.

With every breeze, new dreams are spun,
Carried forth till the day is done.
In whispers soft, we find our way,
Guided by the wind's sweet play.

Petals Adrift on a Spellbound Stream

Petals float on whispers of dreams,
Carried softly by moonlit beams.
Reflections dance in a liquid swirl,
Nature's secrets begin to unfurl.

With each ripple, tales are spun,
Of love and loss, of battles won.
The water sings a timeless song,
Where shadows linger and echoes long.

Colors blend in a symphony bright,
Crafting shadows in the gentle night.
A journey begins on this serene flow,
As petals drift where wild breezes blow.

Beneath the surface, magic brews,
Hidden wonders in vibrant hues.
A world beyond what eyes can see,
Where the heart dances, wild and free.

In this realm of flowing grace,
Time stands still, a sacred space.
Petals adrift, on a spellbound stream,
Woven deep into nature's dream.

Under the Weight of Ancient Leaves

Whispers rustle through the boughs,
Ancient tales in sacred vows.
Leaves that blanket the forest floor,
Guard the secrets of those before.

Each layer holds a story deep,
Silent watchers while others sleep.
Time weaves through the gnarled roots,
In the heart where the past still shoots.

Moss cushions footsteps, soft and light,
Guiding wanderers through fading light.
A gentle hush falls with the dusk,
Nature's breath, an emerald husk.

Branches cradle a sky so vast,
Holding memories, tangled, cast.
Underneath the weight they bare,
Lies the essence of reverent care.

In echoes of leaves, history sways,
Crafting paths of enchanted ways.
Beneath the weight of time's embrace,
Life dances on in this timeless place.

Echoes of Legacy in Every Gnarled Twist

In every twist of bark and vine,
Echoes linger, a tale divine.
Gnarled branches tell stories old,
Of hearts that shaped the world so bold.

Roots that reach down, deep and wide,
Hold the wisdom that they abide.
Time unwinds in a tangled dance,
Breathing life into every chance.

The forest whispers in hushed tones,
Each creak and crack a set of stones.
Legacies carved by nature's hand,
The language of earth, forever grand.

Moss-covered memories softly fade,
Nature's canvas, elegantly laid.
Within each ring and each embrace,
The pulse of life finds its place.

Beneath the surface, stories rise,
In whispered legends of the wise.
Echoes of legacy, steadfast and true,
In every gnarled twist, a journey anew.

Beckoning Ghosts Beneath the Canopy

Ghostly figures in twilight glow,
Dance through shadows where soft winds blow.
Beneath the canopy, whispers sigh,
As ancient memories weave and fly.

The air is thick with tales untold,
Of wanderers lost and brave, bold.
Starlight flickers through verdant leaves,
Entwining dreams that the night weaves.

In the silence, stories unfold,
Of journeys taken, glories and gold.
Soulful echoes call from afar,
Guiding lost hearts where the shadows are.

With every rustle, secrets moan,
Lost souls finding their way back home.
Glimmers of light pierce the dense gloom,
Beckoning spirits to break free from doom.

Under the watchful gaze of night,
Ghosts awaken, ready for flight.
Within the canopy's gentle sway,
They beckon, inviting us to stay.

The Sorcerer's Woven Tapestry

In shadows deep, the threads entwine,
Colors dance with secrets fine.
A spell is cast, a whispered sigh,
Each knot a dream, as hours fly.

Stars emerge from cloaks of night,
Illuminating the sorcerer's sight.
With every pull, a fate is spun,
In silence, magic has begun.

Ancient runes upon the loom,
Binding worlds where echoes bloom.
A tapestry of fate and chance,
Revealing truths in shadow's dance.

Woven visions shift and sway,
Guiding lost souls on their way.
In the threads, a story told,
A tale of courage, brave and bold.

The sorcerer grins, the night unfolds,
As mysteries within him hold.
His woven art, a guiding star,
A map for all, both near and far.

Secrets Beneath a Canopy of Stars

Glimmers shine in velvet skies,
Whispers of dreams as night complies.
Beneath the boughs, a world awaits,
Where magic lingers, and fate creates.

Silvery beams through leaves cascade,
Drawing shadows that softly fade.
Secrets hidden in the glow,
Of starlit stories lost in flow.

Each twinkling light, a distant tale,
Of ancient journeys, soft and pale.
In hushed tones, the silence speaks,
Revealing wonders every week.

Ephemeral moments float on air,
In the heart of nature's care.
Lost in dreams beneath the light,
Where hopes are born and fears take flight.

A dance of dusk and dawn's embrace,
In this canopy, we find our place.
For every star that graces night,
A bond is formed, an endless flight.

Nature's Riddles and Celestial Ties

Whispers crawl through leaves of green,
Nature's riddles, rarely seen.
Questions linger in the breeze,
Echoing through the tallest trees.

Mountains rise with silent grace,
Holding stories time can't erase.
Streams weave paths like woven threads,
Flowing onward where fairness spreads.

Celestial ties in a tapestry,
Stars align in harmony.
Each constellation tells a tale,
Of love and loss, of hope set sail.

Cicadas hum in twilight's glow,
Reminders of the time we sow.
Nature beckons, asks us to seek,
The answers found in the softest peak.

A dance unbroken, old and wise,
Through the ages, the spirit flies.
In nature's arms, we find our way,
Unraveling riddles day by day.

Echoes from the Fractal Land

In fractal realms, dimensions meet,
Patterns swirl in rhythmic beat.
Each echo calls from depth unseen,
Whispers curling, soft and keen.

Mountains rise in mirrored grace,
Each peak reflects its own embrace.
Infinity cradles the skies above,
A canvas where shadows move with love.

Through tangled paths where silence reigns,
Reality shifts, and time wanes.
Explorers tread on ancient stone,
In fractal whispers, we are not alone.

Each step unveils a hidden door,
To places glimpsed but never bore.
The land responds with songs so sweet,
In echoes deep, our hearts repeat.

Release the bounds of what you know,
In fractal land, let spirit flow.
For every echo leads us near,
To truths that rise, to dreams we steer.

The Crown of Nature's Sorcery

In the forest deep, shadows dance,
Leaves whisper secrets, old as chance.
Mossy stones, a carpet lush,
Nature's crown, in silence, hush.

Waves of green wrap around the trees,
Ancient spirits ride the breeze.
Glimmers of gold, a fleeting glance,
Nature's magic in a trance.

Roots entwine where the wild things play,
Under a sky of fading gray.
In twilight hours, mysteries swirl,
The spells of the earth unfurl.

Every blossom, a tale to share,
Carried gently by the air.
Crowned in beauty, wild and free,
Nature's sorcery speaks to me.

In this realm, where time stands still,
The heart of magic, an endless thrill.
Veils of twilight, shadows cast,
The crown of nature, forever vast.

Secrets Woven in Thorny Vines

Beneath the thicket, tangled dreams,
Whispers float in muted screams.
Thorns like sentinels guard the way,
Secrets hidden, come what may.

Buds unfurl in cautious grace,
Nature's wonders, a secret place.
Each twisted stem, a story shared,
Woven tales of love and care.

Moonlight drapes the swaying leaves,
Where the heart believes and grieves.
In shadows deep, the truth will pine,
Desires caught in thorny vine.

Fleeting moments brushed by time,
Echoes linger, soft and prime.
In the hush, the heart is twined,
With every secret, love is blind.

So tread with caution, step with grace,
In the tangle, find your place.
For in the thorns, there's beauty waiting,
Secrets woven, always creating.

Twilight Gardens and Arcane Paths

In twilight gardens, magic hums,
Where the nightingale softly strums.
Petals whisper tales of old,
In the dusk, the stars unfold.

Arcane paths through fragrant blooms,
Guided by the mystic's tunes.
Shadows stretch, the moonlight beams,
Illuminating lovers' dreams.

Beneath the arch of willow bows,
Nature sighs, and softly bows.
Each step brings a new delight,
In the garden, hearts take flight.

Mossy stones tell stories sweet,
Where the earth and magic meet.
In every rustle, every sigh,
The garden's soul will never die.

So wander deep, let your heart roam,
In twilight's glow, you'll find your home.
Arcane paths and blooms entwined,
In the garden of the divine.

The Weaver's Spell Among the Boughs

In ancient woods, where boughs embrace,
A weaver spins, with gentle grace.
Threads of light in twilight glow,
The stories of the forest flow.

Each woven strand, a thread of fate,
Binding worlds, both small and great.
In the cradle of the trees,
Nature sings upon the breeze.

The weaver's hands know every tale,
Of silent dreams and whispered wail.
Among the leaves, the secrets weave,
In every heart, the weaver believes.

Raindrops glisten, catch the light,
As stars awaken, sparkling bright.
In the tapestry of night and day,
The weaver's spell will always stay.

So pause and listen, heed the call,
For in the boughs, there's magic for all.
With every stitch, a legend grows,
In the weaver's world, love overflows.

The Dance of Shadows and Leaves

In the whispering wind they sway,
Shadows twist in gleeful play.
Leaves flutter down, a gentle sigh,
Nature's ballet, high and nigh.

Moonlight kisses the forest's floor,
A symphony of rustling, a soft score.
Branches reach out like hands so free,
Inviting the night's endless spree.

Stars blink down in silent cheer,
As shadows dance, drawing near.
Under a cloak of midnight blue,
The world awakens, vibrant and true.

With every rustle, stories flow,
Of dreams that shimmer and hearts aglow.
Nature's rhythm, a timeless theme,
In the dark, they weave and dream.

Embracing night in wild delight,
Shadows and leaves, hearts take flight.
Together they spin, entwined in grace,
In this embrace, find your place.

Serpentines of Nature's Pall

Winding paths through the twilight,
Nature whispers secrets in the night.
Each twist a tale, each turn a song,
In emerald hues where shadows throng.

Beneath the boughs where spirits tread,
Ancient voices softly spread.
In this realm where echoes play,
The serpentines lead the way.

Rivers shimmer with a ghostly glow,
Reflecting dreams that ebb and flow.
Through tangled roots, life intertwines,
In nature's heart, the sacred shrines.

Mist curls gently, a lover's breath,
Hiding secrets of life and death.
The path may twist, the shadows close,
Yet beauty blooms where darkness goes.

Embrace the wild, the untamed lore,
Each step reveals what came before.
Through serpentines of nature's pall,
Hear the silent, enchanting call.

Under the Gaze of the Enchanted Crow

In the stillness, a shadow flies,
A crow alights with knowing eyes.
Wings spread wide, a darkened sail,
Under his watch, secrets prevail.

Whispers of wisdom in every caw,
Stories unraveled in nature's draw.
Beneath his gaze, time stands still,
Magic dances, bending will.

Branches cradle the midnight hue,
As starlight bathes the world anew.
In silence, dreams begin to grow,
Under the gaze of the enchanted crow.

Time flows softly, like a stream,
Casting shadows on every dream.
In his watch, life finds its way,
Through night's embrace and dawning day.

With every flutter, spirits rise,
Under the spell of ancient skies.
The crow's allure, forever flows,
In whispered tales, the heart bestows.

Verdant Mysteries Locked within Fences

Behind the fences, gardens bloom,
Secrets linger in fragrant gloom.
In emerald whispers, nature speaks,
Where time is paused, and stillness seeks.

Vines climb high, reaching for light,
Guarding tales of day and night.
Petals unfurl, vibrant and bold,
In this haven, mysteries unfold.

Life intertwines in a secret dance,
Each leaf a story, inviting chance.
The air thickens with scented dreams,
Whispers float like gentle streams.

Curious eyes peer through the wood,
Yearning to know the hidden good.
In the lush veil of muted greens,
Lie tales of laughter and faded scenes.

Within these fences, magic lies,
In verdant shades beneath the skies.
Embrace the mysteries, let them chance,
In nature's heart, find your dance.

Riddles Carved in Bark and Stone

Whispers lie within the trees,
Crafted tales by night's cool breeze.
Symbols etched in ancient lore,
Nature speaks, we listen more.

The stones remember what they've seen,
Guarding secrets, calm and keen.
Each grain tells a story bold,
Of time's embrace in shadows cold.

Twists of bark, a puzzle hide,
In every ring, a tale of pride.
Find the path where roots entwine,
And meet the whispers, soft, divine.

The wise owl hoots a riddle deep,
In silent woods, where shadows creep.
Follow closely, heed each sound,
For the truth in nature's found.

In twilight's glow, the riddles play,
Beneath the stars, they softly sway.
Unlock the meanings, let them flow,
In bark and stone, the answers grow.

The Crowned Faery's Domain

In glades where sunlight dances bright,
Faeries play in morning light.
A crown of blooms upon her head,
Among the petals, softly tread.

Whispers float on lilac air,
Magic woven everywhere.
Glistening dew on leaves of green,
In her realm, all is serene.

Fluttering wings like silver dreams,
Laughter spills in silver streams.
Underneath the ancient trees,
Time stands still, a gentle breeze.

Moonlight kisses every flower,
In her presence, breathless power.
Stars above her sparkling throne,
In the night, she reigns alone.

Her subjects, shadows, dance with glee,
In a realm where all are free.
Guardians of the twilight hour,
In her heart, there lies the power.

Secrets Entombed in the Weaving

Threads of fate in shadows spun,
Where time and stories, both are one.
Patterns rich with tales untold,
In every stitch, a world unfolds.

The loom's song hums a soft refrain,
Echoes of joy, whispers of pain.
Lost in the tapestry's embrace,
Every thread, a memory's trace.

Entombed within the woven art,
Lie the secrets of the heart.
Colors blend and softly fade,
In this realm where dreams are made.

Adorned with gems of twilight's hue,
Enchantments weave in shades anew.
Each knot a tale, each fiber a sigh,
Beneath the stars, they float and fly.

In every weave, a journey waits,
From joy and sorrow, love creates.
Pen the story in threads of gold,
For life's great tapestry unfolds.

Nightfall Among Enchanted Roots

As shadows stretch across the ground,
In the hush, a magic found.
Roots entwined in a lover's dance,
Under moonlight, nature's trance.

Silken ribbons of mist arise,
Twinkling soft like distant skies.
Ancient knells of the forest deep,
In this realm, the quiet keeps.

Beneath the canopy, whispers roam,
Every root a story's home.
Tales of the earth, old and wise,
In the night, where mystery lies.

In the dark, soft whispers call,
Promises made among them all.
A gathering of souls entwined,
In the roots, a peace defined.

The stars above, a watchful eye,
Guiding dreams as they softly fly.
Among the earth's enchanted frame,
Nightfall beckons, whispering names.

Mystic Paths Laced with Thorns

In shadows where the thorns do creep,
A winding path that secrets keep.
With every step, the whispers call,
To brave the night, to risk the fall.

The moonlit glow, a fleeting guide,
Through tangled roots where fears reside.
Yet courage singes through the doubt,
And leads the way, a heart devout.

Through brambles thick and shadows deep,
The thorns unveil what dreams can reap.
In every scratch, a lesson learned,
In every scar, a fire burned.

With twilight's breath, the path unfolds,
A journey steeped in tales of old.
Though pricked by pain, resolve still sings,
For on this road, the spirit clings.

So tread with care, but walk with pride,
For mystic paths do not abide.
They swirl like smoke, both fierce and bold,
In thorns, the brave shall find their gold.

Melody Among the Wind-Swept Pines

Beneath the boughs where breezes play,
The pines hum softly, night and day.
Their voices rise in gentle strains,
A melody that softly wanes.

Each needle's sigh, a whispered tune,
A dance beneath the silver moon.
With every rustle, every breeze,
The forest sways, a symphony it frees.

Oh, listen close, the secrets shared,
In every note, a heart laid bare.
Among the trunks, the stories weave,
A tapestry of all who believe.

As shadows dip and daylight fades,
The chorus stirs in twilight shades.
The pines remind us, in the din,
The song of life begins within.

So wander forth and hear the call,
In every whisper, life's enthrall.
Embrace the sound, let spirits soar,
For in the pines, we're evermore.

Fractured Realities in Ancient Hollows

In caverns deep where echoes dwell,
The fractured truths begin to swell.
Each shadow holds a tale untold,
Of lives once lived, now turned to gold.

A flicker here, a whisper there,
The weight of time hangs in the air.
Through ancient halls, the past does roam,
In every crack, a ghostly home.

Reflections shift, realities break,
The strange unveils what dreams can make.
With every breath, the fabric strains,
Of worlds entwined where anything remains.

Among the stones, secrets abide,
In every fissure, truth can hide.
A journey's end, in shades of gray,
Yet hope persists, it lights the way.

So venture forth into the night,
Embrace the darkness, seek the light.
For in these hollowed, ancient spaces,
Fractured worlds reveal their faces.

The Gathering of Forsaken Leaves

When autumn winds begin to sway,
The leaves conspire in disarray.
A dance of colors, bold and bright,
As nature weaves her final rite.

Among the ground, their whispers blend,
In hues of amber, they descend.
A gathering of tales long spent,
In rustling echoes, time is lent.

Each leaf a story, rich and vast,
Of sunlit days and shadows cast.
Together they spin a woven fate,
In unity, they celebrate.

As winds arrive to whisk them near,
The bond they share is pure and clear.
Forsaken yet, they stand so tall,
In every fall, they heed the call.

So let them swirl, in playful flight,
Forsaken leaves, a pure delight.
For in their dance, a truth perceived,
In every end, a life believed.

The Sylvan Sentinel's Oath

In shadows deep, where silence reigns,
The sentinel stands, bound by chains.
With whispers soft, the forest speaks,
He guards the heart, where nature seeks.

Through tangled roots, his vow holds strong,
In twilight's grasp, where shadows long.
To shield the dreams of leaf and stream,
He keeps the night's eternal dream.

With every breath, the oaks shall sway,
As winds of magic drift and play.
By moonlit path, his spirit thrives,
In every pulse, the forest lives.

Forever sworn, beneath the sky,
The watcher waits as seasons fly.
In silence, he holds the verdant wealth,
The sylvan truth, the forest's health.

So pledge we now, in nature's keep,
A bond with roots, both wide and deep.
In harmony, we find our place,
A sacred oath, a wild embrace.

Mirrors of Darkness in Frosty Light

In shadows cast by icy hue,
The world reflects a glacial view.
With whispers low, the night unfolds,
A tapestry of secrets told.

Beneath the stars, the chill winds sigh,
As echoes stir the darkened sky.
With every breath, the frost bites deep,
In silence, secrets dare to creep.

The moon, a ghost in silver lace,
Illuminates a frozen space.
With glimmering shards, the darkness bends,
Mirrors of night where vision ends.

A dance of shadows, sharp and bright,
In frosty realms, we take our flight.
With every step, the echo lingers,
In woven tales, we trace our fingers.

Through frigid air, a whisper calls,
In winter's grasp, the darkness falls.
A paradox of light and shade,
In cosmic reflections, truths are laid.

Branches Scribbled with Arcane Ink

Beneath the boughs where shadows twist,
Arcane tales in silence persist.
With ancient runes on bark inscribed,
The forest breathes, alive, imbibed.

Each leaf a page, a story told,
In whispers soft, of wizards bold.
Branches reach in cryptic dance,
To draw the curious into trance.

A tapestry of night unspun,
The ink of stars, a spell begun.
Within the hush of twilight's kiss,
The secrets weave, a shadowed bliss.

With every sigh, the wood conceals,
The truths that only silence reveals.
In every crack of bark, a line,
Of ancient magic, fierce and divine.

So gather round, both young and old,
For stories rich, and wisdom bold.
With branches scribbled in the dark,
We find our light, we leave a mark.

The Enclave of Thorns and Wonder

In hidden woods, where thorns abound,
An enclave waits, in silence found.
With colors bright, the blossoms spring,
In secret realms, the heart takes wing.

Amidst the brambles, dreams ignite,
A dance of shadows, pure delight.
With tender roots that weave and bind,
In thorns, a sanctuary we find.

The whispers sing of ancient lore,
In every thorn, a key to more.
A hidden realm of wonder grows,
In petals soft, the mystery flows.

With every step, the magic hums,
A calling loud, the forest drums.
In thicket deep, where few have trod,
The enclave breathes, a sacred nod.

So venture forth, the bold and brave,
Amongst the thorns, adventure paves.
In every bloom, a tale's begun,
In wonder's arms, we dream as one.

Twisted Branches of Enchantment

Twisted branches touch the sky,
Their whispers dance, a lullaby.
In twilight's glow, their secrets stay,
Entwined in dreams, they lead the way.

Leaves that shimmer, green and gold,
Stories of magic, yet untold.
Beneath the boughs where shadows creep,
A promise lies, in silence deep.

Twilight spirits begin to play,
With every breeze, they sway and sway.
Through emerald veils, the light does weave,
A tapestry of those who believe.

Moonlit trails of silver hue,
Guide the lost, the brave, the few.
In every twist, a world unseen,
The heart of magic flows between.

With every breath, enchantment stirs,
In twisted paths where nature purrs.
The air is thick with ancient sighs,
As twilight whispers weave the skies.

Shadows Beneath the Ancient Canopy

Shadows dance where daylight fades,
Beneath the boughs, the silence wades.
Roots entwined in earth so deep,
In hidden realms where secrets sleep.

The ancient trees stand tall and wise,
Guardians under starry skies.
Their gnarled limbs embrace the night,
Veils of darkness cloak the light.

Echoes of life in whispers flow,
With every breeze, the stories grow.
In spirit forms, the past awakes,
A symphony that softly shakes.

Mossy carpets, cool and sweet,
Cradle feet that dare to meet.
Nature's breath, a calming balm,
In shadows found, our hearts feel calm.

From ancient roots to leafy crowns,
History lingers, though all surrounding towns.
The magic thrives in quiet guise,
In shadows deep, the truth belies.

Whispers of the Elder Woods

Whispers echo through the trees,
Carried softly on the breeze.
In elder woods where spirits roam,
Nature sings a welcome home.

Branches weave a tale of old,
In every leaf, a story told.
The ground holds memories, rich and vast,
A tapestry of the forgotten past.

Sunlight dapples on the floor,
Illuminating myths and lore.
With every rustle, the woods confide,
Secrets held where shadows hide.

The harmony of life surrounds,
In tranquil sights, the heart abounds.
Glistening dew on emerald beds,
A gentle touch where nature treads.

Echoing songs of gentle streams,
A world alive with whispered dreams.
In elder woods, the spirit flows,
Beneath the skies, enchantment grows.

Mystical Barriers and Enchanted Thorns

Barriers rise, both fierce and grand,
Guarding realms of magic land.
Enchanted thorns like secrets bind,
Protecting wonders yet to find.

Every petal holds a spark,
In colors vivid, brave, and stark.
Through tangled vines, the path unfolds,
To where the heart's desire holds.

Whispers beckon past the gate,
Where dreams and shadows intertwine fate.
A tapestry of light and shade,
In mystical realms where hope is laid.

Brave souls tread with open hearts,
Embracing magic, as life imparts.
Through enchanted thorns, they weave their way,
Where every dusk brings forth the day.

So wander close, yet tread with care,
In enchanted thickets, magic's rare.
Beyond the barriers, wonders gleam,
In whispered tales, the heart will dream.

Grove of the Gloaming Spirits

In twilight's grasp, the shadows play,
Whispers weave through trees so gray.
Softly glows the fading light,
Gloaming spirits dance in flight.

Rustling leaves, a gentle sigh,
Calling forth the night's reply.
Misty trails where echoes dwell,
Lost in dreams, a hidden spell.

Crickets sing their evening song,
As the night unfolds, so long.
Stars awaken, bright and bold,
Tales of wonder, yet untold.

In this grove, where silence thrives,
Every breath, the stillness drives.
Nature's heartbeats pulse so near,
Harmony that calms all fear.

Beneath the boughs, the spirits glide,
In every glimmer, shadows hide.
Grove of dusk, where secrets keep,
In twilight's arms, we softly sleep.

Echoing Heartbeats of the Wild

Beneath the arching boughs we stand,
The pulse of the earth, soft and grand.
Whispers ride on the evening breeze,
Nature's heart, a rhythmic tease.

Footfalls echo on the ground,
In the stillness, life abounds.
Rustling grasses, stories told,
In the wild, hearts turn to gold.

Moonlit paths invite our gaze,
In this realm, we weave our ways.
With every step, the heartbeat flows,
Unity in nature grows.

Gentle creatures pass us by,
In quiet moments, spirits fly.
Echoes linger, soft as air,
Through the wild, we find our care.

In the forest's breath, we trust,
Among the leaves, the ancient dust.
With every echo, life ignites,
Heartbeats dance in wild delights.

The Ballet of Bearded Branches

In twilight's glow, the branches sway,
Bearded leaves in soft display.
Each movement tells a tale of yore,
A ballet held on nature's floor.

Draped in moss, a waltz so slow,
Leaves pirouette, the moonlight's show.
Whispers tickle the evening air,
A dance of dreams, beyond compare.

Rooted deep in ancient lore,
Branches bow, and spirits soar.
With every twist, a song is spun,
The ballet breathes, we come undone.

Stars like dancers in the night,
Swaying softly, bold and bright.
Nature's grace, an endless flow,
A tapestry of life aglow.

In this grand performance's hold,
Every flicker, every fold.
The bearded branches sway and twine,
In harmony, we find the divine.

Enshrined in Nature's Woven Spell

Amidst the leaves, a magic hums,
In every corner, nature drums.
Woven whispers in the air,
Enshrined in beauty, beyond compare.

Sunbeams filter through the green,
Casting warmth, a golden sheen.
Petals glisten, dew-kissed bright,
In this sanctuary of light.

Birdsongs weave a tapestry,
Flowing free, a symphony.
Roots entwined in earth's embrace,
In this haven, we find our place.

Mysterious shadows dance and twirl,
Nature's secrets begin to unfurl.
With every breath, we feel the call,
Enshrined in grace, we rise, we fall.

In nature's arms, our spirits blend,
A woven spell that knows no end.
Here we gather, hearts laid bare,
Enshrined in love, we breathe the air.

The Elven Tapestry Under the Moon

Beneath the moon's soft, silver gaze,
Elven whispers weave through night.
Threads of magic, ancient ways,
In starlit dance, their hearts take flight.

With every stitch, a story spun,
Of shadows deep and light that gleams.
In forests where the rivers run,
They foster dreams, weaving dreams.

Through branches high and leaves that sway,
Mysteries linger, secrets kept.
In the night, the elves will play,
As timeless stars in silence slept.

From every corner, echoes call,
Of laughter light and echoes lost.
They build a bridge, a vivid wall,
Between the worlds, where worlds are tossed.

So gather close, beneath the sky,
Feel the magic in the air.
Let not the fleeting moment fly,
For in this night, all souls lay bare.

Crowned Figures in the Mist

In the mist where shadows dwell,
Figures gather, crowned in dreams.
With whispers soft, they weave a spell,
A haunting dance that gently gleams.

Each crown adorned with stories old,
Of kings and queens, of loss and grace.
Their eyes hold secrets, bright and bold,
Reflections of a forgotten place.

Through veils of fog and muted light,
They wander softly, hearts entwined.
Crowned figures, shrouded in the night,
Leaving echoes for the minds they bind.

With every step, the world awakes,
A tapestry of fate does show.
What path to tread, what choice it makes,
In misty realms where time doth flow.

So heed the call, embrace the mist,
As crowned figures dance and sway.
Their legacy is not but tryst,
In dreams that linger, night to day.

The Sorcerer's Briar

In depths of woods where shadows sigh,
A briar grows, both fierce and wild.
The sorcerer walks with watchful eye,
Guarding secrets, nature's child.

With thorny reach and vibrant bloom,
It sings of power wrapped in pain.
In silence deep, it casts a gloom,
A path to magic, tethered chain.

Each prick reveals a wisdom lost,
A dance of light through bramble dark.
To wander here, one pays the cost,
For every wish ignites a spark.

Through tangled roots and whispered lore,
The sorcerer's heart knows every tale.
In briar realms where spirits soar,
Resilience blooms, through winds that wail.

So tread with care on paths unseen,
For magic flows in every breath.
The sorcerer's briar, fierce yet keen,
In every thorn, a dance with death.

Tales of the Whispering Wild

In realms where wild things roam and sing,
Whispers curl in the cool night air.
Tales unfold, as shadows cling,
Of heartbeats lost and souls laid bare.

Among the trees, secrets hide deep,
Of wanderers and dreams unchained.
The wild holds promises to keep,
In softest sighs where hope is gained.

Each rustling leaf, a story told,
Of nature's dance in gentle grace.
In twilight's haze, the fears unfold,
And wild hearts find their rightful place.

Through emerald paths that twist like fate,
The whispering wild calls true and clear.
A beckoning that cannot wait,
For every journey holds its cheer.

So step with care, embrace the sound,
Of nature's lore, where dreams abide.
In tales of wild, true magic's found,
As whispers blend with the rising tide.

Charms Hidden in the Underbrush

Beneath the leaves, a sparkle lies,
A whispered spell beneath the skies.
Soft shadows dance on ancient ground,
Where secrets of the forest abound.

Thorns entwine with blooms so rare,
In hidden nooks, enchantments flare.
Silent watchers, trees embrace,
Guard the magic in this place.

Mossy carpets, a quiet tread,
With every step, old tales are bred.
Creeping vines and stories told,
In the underbrush, the charms unfold.

Faint echoes of a long-lost song,
Fate and fortune can't be wrong.
In the shadows, spirits hover,
Calling hearts to seek each other.

So linger here, let time stand still,
Where woodland whispers bend your will.
The essence of the earth, you'll feel,
In the charms, the forest's reel.

Crowns of Twisted Fate

Amid the thorns, the roses bloom,
A monarch's heart can seal its doom.
Crowned in shadows, fate takes flight,
Beneath the stars, a woeful night.

Threads of silver, whispers weave,
In the silence, mourners grieve.
Destinies forged in quiet sighs,
Crafted in the darkened skies.

Glimmers dance on woven crowns,
Crown of thorns and jeweled frowns.
Lifted high, yet tethered low,
By the path that one must go.

In the tangle of fate's embrace,
Hearts entwined in strands misplace.
Blindly trusting what's unseen,
Each twist reveals a hidden glean.

So wear your crown with cautious grace,
For every choice leaves a trace.
In shadows deep, where fates collide,
The twisting paths may turn the tide.

Where Magic Meets the Thicket

In thickets dense, the secrets stir,
Where magic weaves like softest fur.
With every rustle, stories climb,
In whispers of the ancient rhyme.

Beneath the canopy, light plays tricks,
A tapestry of nature's picks.
Crimson berries, twilight's kiss,
In this realm, you can't miss.

Fleeting shadows dart with grace,
In every nook, a hidden place.
Fluttering wings, a gentle sound,
Where enchantments leap and abound.

The heartbeats of the woodland blend,
In harmony, the realms extend.
Magic mingles with the dark,
A vibrant life, a glowing spark.

So wander here, where spirits roam,
In the thicket, you will find home.
Each step unveils a wonder's thread,
As dreams awaken, softly spread.

The Throne of Nature's Secrets

In the grove, a throne of stone,
Nature's whispers, soft and lone.
Covered in moss, a regal seat,
Holding tales of time and heat.

Roots entwined, a tapestry,
Of life and death, eternity.
Each grain of dirt, a story spun,
Of battles lost and victories won.

From the throne, the world unfurls,
Beneath the stars, the universe swirls.
With every glance, a vision gained,
In nature's heart, nothing's constrained.

Shade and light in a dance so grand,
Holding wonders in its hand.
Every flutter tells a tale,
As secrets breathe upon the gale.

So take a seat and close your eyes,
Feel the magic, let it rise.
For in this throne of nature's grace,
Lies the truth of every place.

Entangled Fables of the Forest

In whispers where the shadows creep,
The ancient tales of nature sleep.
Each leaf a story waiting to be found,
In the tangled roots beneath the ground.

Beneath the boughs where silence reigns,
The echoes of the past remain.
With every rustle, the woods confide,
The fables woven in their stride.

A deer glides softly through the mist,
Embracing moments none could resist.
The songs of night by owls declared,
In twilight's grasp, all dreams are shared.

A fox peers out from shadows deep,
Guarding the secrets the forest keeps.
With eyes aglow, it prowls the night,
Entangled fables take their flight.

Through tangled vines and branches wide,
The lore of ages can't divide.
For every step we take today,
The forest breathes its tales away.

A Court of Leaves and Voices

In the twilight, whispers grow,
A court of leaves, a gentle flow.
With laughter light and secrets shared,
The winds of change bring hearts declared.

Around the roots, soft echoes play,
In colors bright, they dance and sway.
The trees hold counsel, wise and grand,
In nature's court, we take our stand.

Caught in the web of every breeze,
Voices call from ancient trees.
They tell of love, they weave our fate,
In this embrace, we celebrate.

On pathways strewn with golden light,
The creatures gather, day to night.
Each leaf a witness, every sigh,
In harmony, where dreams can fly.

In nature's lore we find our song,
In every heart, we all belong.
The leaves bear witness to the tale,
As winds of time begin to sail.

The Hidden Crown of the Thicket

Deep in the thicket, secrets reign,
A crown forgotten, wrapped in grain.
Where shadows play and light retreats,
The whispers of the forest greet.

Underneath where sunlight fails,
The hidden beauty softly pales.
Each twig and leaf a royal guise,
The majesty in nature lies.

A brook meanders, clear and bright,
Reflecting stars that grace the night.
Its gentle song, a lover's call,
In every droplet, echoes fall.

The foxglove blooms, a regal sight,
Adorning pathways with pure delight.
Among the thorns, the crown is found,
In thicket's heart, where dreams abound.

With every breeze through branches twined,
The whispers of the thicket bind.
A tale of glory, wrapped in green,
The hidden crown remains unseen.

Twisted Timbers Beckoning the Lost

In twisted timbers, shadows loom,
Beckoning wanderers to their doom.
With branches bent in a starry trance,
They whisper secrets, inviting chance.

The path is winding, fraught with doubt,
Yet in the dark, there's light about.
A flickering glow among the trees,
Encourages hearts to venture, please.

Through leaves that shimmer, lost souls tread,
Following voices, echoes ahead.
Each step a shiver, a call to roam,
In twisted timbers, they find their home.

With every breath, the forest sighs,
Revealing truths behind disguise.
In tangled roots, fate intertwines,
Forging a bond that brightly shines.

The night reveals its hidden grace,
In shadows cast, we find our space.
Twisted timbers hold their cost,
Yet they embrace all who are lost.

9 781805 599968